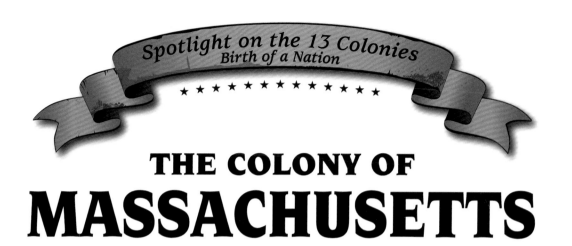

Spotlight on the 13 Colonies
Birth of a Nation

THE COLONY OF
MASSACHUSETTS

Harper Avett

PowerKiDS
press™

NEW YORK

Published in 2016 by The Rosen Publishing Group, Inc.
29 East 21st Street, New York, NY 10010

Editor: Caitie McAneney
Book Design: Andrea Davison-Bartolotta

Photo Credits: Cover DEA Picture Library/Getty Images; p. 5 Albert Bierstadt/Wikimedia Commons; pp. 6–7 American School/Getty Images; p. 8 Jean Leon Gerome Ferris/Library of Congress/Wikimedia Commons; p. 9 courtesy of Library of Congress; p. 11 Everett Historical/Shutterstock.com; p. 12 Hulton Archive/Getty Images; p. 13 Universal History Archive/UIG/Getty Images; pp. 14, 18–19, 21 Stock Montage/Getty Images; pp. 15, 17 North Wind Picture Archives; p.19 (inset) MPI/Stringer/Getty Images; p. 22 VectorPic/Shutterstock.com.

Library of Congress Cataloging-in-Publication Data

Avett, Harper.
The colony of Massachusetts / by Harper Avett.
p. cm. — (Spotlight on the 13 colonies: Birth of a nation)
Includes index.
ISBN 978-1-4994-0511-8 (pbk.)
ISBN 978-1-4994-0512-5 (6 pack)
ISBN 978-1-4994-0519-4 (library binding)
1. Massachusetts — History — Colonial period, ca. 1600 - 1775 — Juvenile literature. 2. Massachusetts — History — 1775 - 1865 — Juvenile literature. I. Avett, Harper. II. Title.
F67.A94 2016
974.4/02—d23

Manufactured in the United States of America

CPSIA Compliance Information: Batch #WS15PK: For further information contact Rosen Publishing, New York, New York at 1-800-237-9932.

Contents

Discovering Massachusetts 4

Finding Freedom 6

Plymouth Colony. 8

The Puritan Way 10

Tension Brews 12

Trading Takes Off 14

Clashing with the King 16

Colonists for Liberty 18

The Revolution Begins 20

The Sixth State 22

Glossary 23

Index 24

Primary Source List 24

Websites 24

Discovering Massachusetts

Massachusetts is a state that's full of natural beauty and history. Its location on the Atlantic coast made it the place the Pilgrims decided to settle. Later, it was the location of the Massachusetts Bay Colony and the home of the American Revolution.

Before Massachusetts was a colony, it was home to Algonquian-speaking Indian tribes. "Algonquian" is commonly used to talk about any of the dozens of different Native American tribes in North America who spoke related languages. The Wampanoag, Mohican, and Mohegan tribes lived in the area that's now Massachusetts. One of the Wampanoag tribes was named the Massachusett. In Algonquian, this word means "by the range of hills."

In 1602, English explorer Bartholomew Gosnold sailed along Cape Cod, on the coast of today's Massachusetts. He also explored Nantucket Sound and an island he named Martha's Vineyard. Gosnold named Cape Cod after the many fish he found there. He named Martha's Vineyard after his daughter, Martha.

This painting shows Bartholomew Gosnold's ship sailing near Cuttyhunk Island, Massachusetts. He and his men built a basic fort there.

5

Finding Freedom

The Plymouth Company first needed to gather a group of people to settle in New England. Finding people willing to move to an unknown land was hard. However, the Plymouth Company soon found a group of people looking for religious freedom from England—Separatists who wanted to break from the Church of England. In this time, it was illegal to think the Church of England was wrong. The Separatists originally tried settling in the Netherlands, but later searched for a place of their own to practice their religion. Together with regular craftsmen, skilled workers, servants, and their families, they formed a group known as the Pilgrims.

The Pilgrims called the place they landed Plymouth Rock. This picture shows the Pilgrims **disembarking** the *Mayflower* to explore the land. Ten years later, another religious group called the Puritans would land near Salem, Massachusetts.

In September 1620, a group of around 100 Pilgrims sailed from England on a ship called the *Mayflower*. They were originally trying to land near the colony of Virginia, which was founded in 1607. Instead, a storm blew them off course. They landed in the area that is today Cape Cod, Massachusetts, on November 11, 1620.

Plymouth Colony

Before the Pilgrims landed, they made a **document** that outlined how their government would work. This document, called the Mayflower Compact, was the first government document of its kind in the English colonies. It was made to keep the peace between Separatist and non-Separatist Pilgrims in the colony. Every adult male on board the *Mayflower*, including William Brewster, William Bradford, and Myles Standish, signed the

signing the
Mayflower Compact

document. The Mayflower Compact is a great example of early American **democracy**.

After signing the Mayflower Compact, a group of men left the *Mayflower* and explored the lands nearby to find a place to settle. Nearly a month later, the rest of the Pilgrims landed in Plymouth Harbor and started building their colony.

The first winter was very **difficult**. Half the Pilgrims died from hunger and sickness. In the spring, friendly Wampanoag and Narragansett Indians taught the colonists how to catch fish and plant native crops, such as beans and corn.

After the Pilgrims' crops were harvested in the fall, the Native Americans had a feast with them. This is known as the first Thanksgiving.

The Puritan Way

The Massachusetts Bay Colony obtained a charter from King Charles I to settle in Massachusetts in 1629. In 1630, nearly 1,000 Puritans left England under the leadership of Governor John Winthrop.

Separatists weren't the only Englishmen looking for religious freedom. Puritans believed people should live simple lives centered on faith. They wanted to make the Church of England pure by ridding it of Catholic practices. Puritan government was based on God, and going to church was **mandatory**. There were severe punishments for those who sinned. Religious leaders, such as Reverend Cotton Mather, were very powerful.

In the decade that followed, thousands more came to the colony, including merchants hoping to make money through trade. Plymouth Colony became a part of the Massachusetts Bay Colony in 1691. Colonists built new towns, such as Boston, which was founded in 1630. America's first public school, called Boston Latin School, opened in Boston in 1635. Harvard University in Boston became America's first college in 1636.

Salem Witch Trial, 1692

The Puritans believed it was their duty to rid their colony of evil, especially witchcraft. In 1692, a group of young girls accused local men and women of witchcraft. During the Salem Witch Trials, some of the accused were thrown into prison, while others were hanged or worse.

Tension Brews

When settlers first arrived, native tribes in Massachusetts were friendly. They were willing to help colonists learn to farm and even shared their land. But **tension** began to grow when colonists wanted the land for themselves. Soon, colonists believed they owned the land, and they forced native peoples from it. Natives could no longer hunt or farm on land they had used for centuries. Some had to work for the colonists on their farms. They became dependent on the colonists for food and weapons. It seemed the colonists were now in charge of the land that had always belonged to the native tribes.

In 1675, a war known as King Philip's War broke out between native tribes and colonists. Native tribes such as the Wampanoag and Narragansett banded together to fight colonists. They were led by Chief Metacomet, known to the colonists as King Philip. The fighting raged for 14 months, until colonists captured Metacomet and killed him. Many natives who survived were punished through slavery and loss of land.

Chief Metacomet

This picture shows the Battle of Bloody Brook, which was fought in September 1675. In this battle, natives **ambushed** colonists near present-day Deerfield, Massachusetts.

Trading Takes Off

Winters were long and rough, and tension with Native Americans was difficult. However, by the late 1600s, colonists in Massachusetts were starting to see success. Towns were growing and becoming more modern, thanks to skilled workers, such as brickmakers, carpenters, and blacksmiths. The Massachusetts Bay Colony began producing enough lumber, beef, and fur to **export** to England and its colonies in the Caribbean. Colonists built more ships, which made trading and fishing easier.

Ports in Massachusetts became a key part of a trading network called the triangle trade. Colonists exported rum to Africa in exchange for slaves, who were brought over on small, dirty ships. Slaves were traded in the West Indies for sugar to make more rum. Massachusetts became the first New England colony to use slave labor. Some slaves in Massachusetts worked on farms, but most worked as servants or laborers for merchants or tradesmen. Famous former slaves from Massachusetts include the poet Phillis Wheatley and activist Mum Bett.

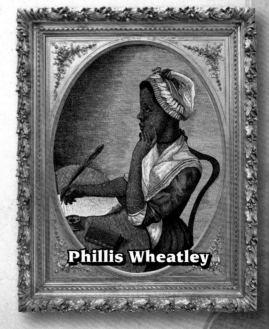

Phillis Wheatley

This illustration depicts an office for a colonial shipping business.

Clashing with the King

As the colonists expanded their trade and created their own **identity**, they became more independent from England. However, they were still under British control. In the mid-1700s, this became a problem as England raised taxes on the colonists.

King George III of England believed the colonies should help pay for the French and Indian War. This was a war fought from 1754 to 1763 between Britain and France for territory in America. England needed money to pay for the war and to keep the peace between colonists and Native Americans on the western frontier.

In 1764, King George and **Parliament** passed the Sugar Act, which put a tax on sugar products. This hurt the colonies' trade, which greatly angered the colonists. Unlike citizens living in England, colonists couldn't vote for **representatives** in Parliament. The colonists called for "no taxation without representation." The colonists boycotted, or refused to buy, sugar under the Sugar Act. It was one of the first acts of colonial **rebellion**.

THE FOLLY OF ENGLAND
AND THE RUIN OF AMERICA

In 1765, England passed the Stamp Act, which taxed paper goods. In August 1765, angry colonists in Boston hung a dummy of Andrew Oliver—the local stamp master—as a sign of protest from a tree, which became known as the Liberty Tree. Angry colonists also burned stamps and refused to use them.

Colonists for Liberty

Boston, Massachusetts, became the center of prerevolutionary tension. The Sons of Liberty was a group of men in Boston who came together to discuss and protest unfair laws. They became known as "patriots."

This illustration shows colonists clashing with British soldiers in the bloody Boston **Massacre**.

Tension rose on March 5, 1770, when a group of British soldiers fought with a group of colonists. Five colonists—including former slave Crispus Attucks—were killed, and the event became known as the Boston Massacre. This event was one of the sparks that started the American Revolution.

The Boston Tea Party was another protest in the years leading up to the war. The Sons of Liberty decided to protest a tax Parliament put on **imported** tea. On December 16, 1773, they boarded three ships in Boston Harbor and threw 342 cases of tea into the water. To punish the colonists, Parliament passed the **Coercive** Acts, which the colonists called the **Intolerable** Acts, in 1774. These acts took more colonial power away and made tension even worse.

▼ **Boston Tea Party**

The Revolution Begins

It soon became clear that England's unfair treatment was only getting worse. On September 5, 1774, leaders from all colonies except Georgia met in Philadelphia, Pennsylvania. This became known as the Continental Congress. The leaders discussed ways they could protest England's actions.

On April 19, 1775, the first battles of the American Revolution took place between colonists and British soldiers at Lexington and Concord in Massachusetts. On June 17, 1775, the Battle of Bunker Hill took place near Boston, Massachusetts. The colonists lost the Battle of Bunker Hill, but it was a brave fight that showed the power of the colonial army.

Colonists became aware that breaking with England was their only chance at freedom. The Second Continental Congress met in May 1775, led by John Hancock of Massachusetts. On July 4, 1776, Congress approved the Declaration of Independence, which stated that the American colonies had the right to freedom from England. In other words, America had become an independent nation.

The night before the Battles of Lexington and Concord, Paul Revere and other horsemen rode through towns in Massachusetts, warning patriots about the British attack.

The Sixth State

Even though America declared its independence, it still had a war to win. Meanwhile, America built a set of laws called the Articles of Confederation to govern the new country. **Ratified** on March 1, 1781, this document gave most power to the colony-states. Each of these bodies—no longer a colony, but not yet a state—made its own constitution to explain the rights and responsibilities of its citizens.

In September and October 1779, the Massachusetts Constitutional Convention met to draft the Massachusetts Constitution. John Hancock was president of the convention. The Massachusetts Constitution of 1780 set up two lawmaking bodies—the House of Representatives and the Senate. Citizens could vote for the lawmaking leaders and the governor.

The American Revolution officially ended in 1783, and America became a free nation. In 1787, representatives met in Philadelphia to improve the Articles of Confederation. They wound up writing a new constitution, and the meetings were called the Constitutional Convention. Massachusetts approved the U.S. Constitution on February 6, 1788. The land of Pilgrims, patriots, and revolutionary protests had become the sixth state.

MASSACHUSETTS

Glossary

ambush: To lie in wait for and attack by surprise.

coercive: Using force to make people do things against their will.

democracy: A government by the people.

difficult: Hard to overcome.

disembark: To go ashore from a ship or boat.

document: A piece of written matter that provides information or that serves as an official record.

export: To send something to another country or place.

identity: Who a person or group is.

imported: Brought in from another country or place.

intolerable: Something that is considered bad and won't be accepted, or tolerated.

mandatory: Something one must do.

massacre: The act of killing a large number of people in a cruel way.

Parliament: The group in England that makes the country's laws.

ratify: To formally approve something.

rebellion: Going against a person or group that's in charge.

representative: A member of a lawmaking body who acts for voters.

tension: A state of unrest or opposition between individuals or groups.

Index

A
American Revolution, 4, 19, 20, 22
Articles of Confederation, 22

B
Battle of Bunker Hill, 20
Battles of Lexington and Concord, 20, 21
Boston, 10, 17, 18, 19, 20
Boston Massacre, 18, 19
Boston Tea Party, 19

C
Coercive Acts, 19
Constitutional Convention, 22
Continental Congress, 20

D
Declaration of Independence, 20

F
French and Indian War, 16

G
Gosnold, Bartholomew, 4, 5

H
Hancock, John, 20, 22

I
Intolerable Acts, 19

K
King Philip's War, 12

M
Massachusett (tribe), 4
Massachusetts Bay Colony, 4, 10, 14
Mayflower, 6, 7, 8
Mayflower Compact, 8
Metacomet, 12

N
Narragansett, 8, 12

P
Pilgrims, 4, 6, 7, 8, 9, 22
Plymouth Colony, 8, 10
Plymouth Company, 6
Plymouth Rock, 6
Puritans, 6, 10, 11

S
Salem, 6, 11
Separatists, 6, 8, 10
slaves, 14, 19

Sons of Liberty, 18, 19
Stamp Act, 17
Sugar Act, 16

T
taxes, 16, 17, 19
triangle trade, 14

U
U.S. Constitution, 22

W
Wampanoag, 4, 8, 12
Wheatley, Phillis, 14

Primary Source List

Cover *Vue de Boston.* Created by Franz Xaver Habermann. Hand-colored etching on paper. 1770s.

p. 14 *Phillis Wheatley, Negro Servant to Mr. John Wheatley, of Boston.* Created by Scipio Moorhead. Hand-colored engraving. From a book of her poems published in 1773 in London, United Kingdom.

p. 19 (inset) *Americans Throwing the Cargoes of the Teaships into the River, at Boston.* Engraving. *In The History of North America*, by W. D. Cooper. Published in 1789 in London, England.

Websites

Due to the changing nature of Internet links, PowerKids Press has developed an online list of websites related to the subject of this book. This site is updated regularly. Please use this link to access the list: www.powerkidslinks.com/s13c/mass